P9-AOB-257

DEC '93

W.

Cousteau

LITTLE SIMON

Simon & Schuster Building, Rockefeller Center

1230 Avenue of the Americas, New York, New York 10020

Copyright © 1991 by Hachette, France and The Cousteau Society, Inc. English translation
copyright © 1993 by The Cousteau Society, Inc. First U.S. edition 1993. All rights reserved
including the right of reproduction in whole or in part in any form. Originally published
in France by Hachette Jeunesse as *ALBATROS*. LITTLE SIMON and colophon are trademarks of
Simon & Schuster.

Manufactured in Singapore   10   9   8   7   6   5   4   3   2   1

CREDITS·

The Cousteau Society, Jacques-Yves Cousteau, Jean-Michel Cousteau

Authors: Pamela Stacey, Christine Causse. Photo Editor: Judy K. Brody

Translation: Jeannine C. Morgan. Project Director: Pamela Stacey, Lesley D. High

With special thanks to: André Demaison, Thierry Piantanida, Veronique Platt, François Sarano.
Photographers: François Sarano, Jean-Michel Cousteau, Jack Grove / Tom Stack & Associates,
The Cousteau Society.

Library of Congress Cataloging-in-Publication Data

Albatros. English, Albatross / the Cousteau Society.   p.   cm.   Summary: Examines the
physical characteristics, behavior, and life cycle of the albatross.   1. Albatrosses—Juvenile
literature.   [1. Albatrosses.]   I. Cousteau Society.   II. Title.   QL696.P63A4313   1993
598.4′2—dc20   92-34179   CIP

ISBN 0-671-86565-X

The Cousteau Society

ALBATROSS

LITTLE SIMON

Published by Simon & Schuster

New York London Toronto Sydney Tokyo Singapore

ALBATROSS

Weight and size
30–37 inches long
6–8 feet wingspan
4.5–6.5 lbs.

Life span
Approximately 80 years

Food
Squid, fish, and krill

Reproduction
Lays one egg every year
One partner for life
Egg hatches after 80 days

Lives in the South Seas
between 60 and 25 degrees south latitude

Can fly for months without landing

Declining population

The albatross flies majestically above the water for months at a time.

With its wings spread the albatross is six feet wide, gliding and soaring high in the sky.

After a long journey it finally lands. It searches for its mate among thousands of other birds.

All its life, the albatross is faithful to one partner.

Reunited at last! The two companions find each other after being separated for a whole year.

Carefully, they groom each other's feathers. They are getting ready for a big event.

With mud and sticks, together they build a nest shaped like a volcano.

Plop! The egg is in the nest. Both mother and father take turns keeping it warm.

Eighty days later, a little bird hatches. The baby grows quickly.

The parent feeds fish to the hungry baby from deep in its beak.

The little albatross is clumsy, but it learns quickly.
Soon it will learn to fly.

Ready for takeoff! The albatross runs very fast and flaps its wings. Then it flies away to begin a new journey.

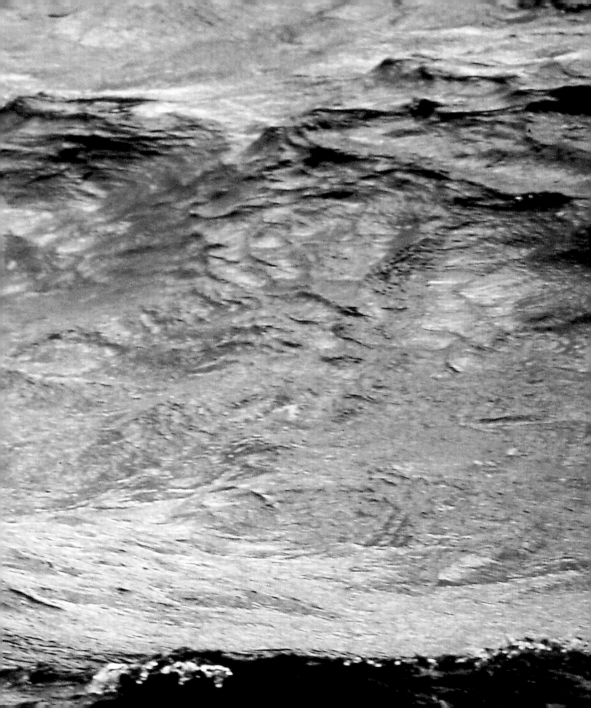